Clap, Clap, Clap

by Lada Josefa Kratky

NATIONAL GEOGRAPHIC

School Publishing

Sunday	Monday	Tuesday	Wednesday	Thursday	Friday	Saturday
1	2	3	4	5	6	7
8	9	10 ☆	11	12	13	14
15	16	17	18	19	20	21
22	23	24	25	26	27	28
29	30					

I see a [calendar].

calendar

I see a 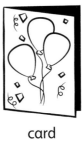.

card

I see a  .

clown

I see a  .

piñata

I see a .

candle

I see a  .

cake

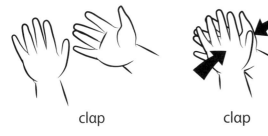

clap   clap   clap